IMPRESSIONS *of the*

SOUTHWEST

of England

Produced by AA Publishing
© Automobile Association Developments Limited 2007

Published by AA Publishing (a trading name of Automobile Association
Developments Limited, whose registered office is Fanum House, Basing View,
Basingstoke, Hampshire RG21 4EA; registered number 1878835)

ISBN-10: 0-7495-5213-1
ISBN-13: 978-0-7495-5213-8

A03033B

A CIP catalogue record for this book is available from the British Library.

Colour reproduction by KDP, Kingsclere
Printed and bound in Thailand by Sirivatana Interprint Public Co Ltd

Opposite: St Michael's Mount, west Cornwall.

IMPRESSIONS *of the*

SOUTHWEST

of England

Picture Acknowledgements

The Automobile Association would like to thank the following photographers, companies
and picture libraries for their assistance in the preparation of this book.

Abbreviations for the picture credits are as follows: (AA) AA World Travel Library

3 AA/Caroline Jones; 5 AA/John Wood; 7 AA/Nigel Hicks; 8 AA/Adam Burton; 9 AA/Adam Burton; 10 AA/Max
Jourdan; 11 AA/John Wood; 12 AA/Max Jourdan; 13 AA/Rupert Tenison; 14 AA/John Wood; 15 AA/Nigel Hicks; 16
AA/James A Tims; 17 AA/Steve Day; 18 AA/John Wood; 19 AA/Adam Burton; 20 AA/John Wood; 21 AA/John Wood;
22 AA/Nigel Hicks; 23 AA/John Wood; 24 AA/Nigel Hicks; 25 AA/Nigel Hicks; 26 AA/John Wood; 27 AA/Nigel
Hicks; 28 AA/Caroline Jones; 29 AA/John Wood; 30 AA/V Sinhal; 31 AA/Adam Burton; 32 AA/Rick Czaja; 33
AA/Nigel Hicks; 34 AA/Nigel Hicks; 35 AA/John Wood; 36 AA/John Wood; 37 AA/John Wood; 38 AA/Nigel Hicks;
39 AA/John Wood; 40 AA/Nigel Hicks; 41 AA/John Wood; 42 AA/Nigel Hicks; 43 AA; 44 AA/John Wood; 45
AA/John Wood; 46 AA/Adam Burton; 47 AA/Nigel Hicks; 48 AA/John Wood; 49 AA/John Wood; 50 AA/Richard
Moss; 51 AA/John Wood; 52 AA/John Wood; 53 AA/John Wood; 54 AA/Eric Meacher; 55 AA/Nigel Hicks; 56
AA/Nigel Hicks; 57 AA/Adam Burton; 58 AA/Nigel Hicks; 59 AA/Nigel Hicks; 60 AA/Nigel Hicks; 61 AA/John
Wood; 62 AA/John Wood; 63 AA/Caroline Jones; 64 AA/Nigel Hicks; 65 AA/John Wood; 66 AA/John Wood; 67
AA/Nigel Hicks; 68 AA/Nigel Hicks; 69 AA/John Wood; 70 AA/Adam Burton; 71 AA/Nigel Hicks; 72 AA/John
Wood; 73 AA/John Wood; 74 AA/Adam Burton; 75 AA/John Wood; 76 AA/Adam Burton; 77 AA/Nigel Hicks; 78
AA/Caroline Jones; 79 AA/John Wood; 80 AA/John Wood; 81 AA/John Wood; 82 AA/Nigel Hicks; 83 AA/R Tennison;
84 AA/John Wood; 85 AA/John Wood; 86 AA/Nigel Hicks; 87 AA/Nigel Hicks; 88 AA/Nigel Hicks; 89 AA/James A
Tims; 90 AA/Nigel Hicks; 91 AA/Max Jourdan; 92 AA/John Wood; 93 AA/Nigel Hicks; 94 AA/John Wood; 95
AA/Adam Burton.

Every effort has been made to trace the copyright holders, and we apologise in advance for any unintentional omissions
or errors. We would be happy to apply the corrections in any following edition of this publication.

Opposite: boats tethered in the shelter of the Fal estuary.

INTRODUCTION

The southwest of England sticks its long finger into the Atlantic Ocean, some 200 miles (322km) from Bristol in the north and Bournemouth in the south. The third point in this triangle is made up by Land's End in west Cornwall, and the scenery there could not be more different from the peninsula's eastern fringes. Here, massive granite cliffs tower above glistening coves of sand and the raging Atlantic swell is an ever-present influence. This far western world is one of legendary mermaids, of Arthurian myths and tales of smugglers. It was also the home of hardy fishermen, miners and quarrymen, whose graft supplied the building blocks for Britain's industrial expansion in the 19th century. Modern Cornwall is less industrial, benign yachters and surfers providing a new employment backbone. The great china clay workings have been replaced by the remarkable giant greenhouses of the Eden Project, a 21st-century solution to the problems of sustainability.

Over the border in Devon, the scenery is a little gentler but no less beautiful. The heatherclad moors of Exmoor and Dartmoor represent the highest land in southern England. Their tors and beacons are the haunt of horse riders and climbers as well as popular walking destinations. Below Dartmoor the west's great port city of Plymouth is just one of the region's maritime gems, with its connections with Raleigh and the voyage to the New World. This south coast is a delight to explore, as wooded creeks and inlets give way to Dorset's 'Jurassic Coast', a UNESCO World Heritage Site for its important fossilised remains from the age of the dinosaurs.

North Devon's coast continues the theme from its Cornish neighbour, with cliffs and airy coastal paths connecting remote harbours and quaint fishing villages. Crossing the boundary into Somerset, high up on Exmoor's plateau, the scenery gently subsides, to rise again only slightly with the Mendip Hills before plunging into the valley of the River Avon. In a gentle hollow at the tip of Somerset, the city of Bath blooms like an exotic flower. Where the Romans celebrated the warm, bubbling spring water, so the dandies of the Georgian century built their grand terraces and parades. Today the city is a vibrant mix of Celtic fringe and cosmopolitan chic.

But above all else, the southwest of England is about the sea. That might mean buckets and spades on one of the many beautiful beaches, or it might mean racing a dinghy around the sheltered waters of a tidal inlet. The growth of the surfing community around Newquay has been a surprise to those who equated the sport with Hawaii, Bondi or California. But here are some of the best waves to be found in Europe and the appeal has spread.

There are of course the regulation pretty villages and clotted cream teas to be had: Devon and Dorset in particular boast more than their fair share of thatchery and rose bedecked cottages. But there is such a wealth of culture and scenery in this region that it would be a shame to dismiss it as simply 'chocolate-box'.

The tower of St Pancras parish church is a distinctive landmark over Widecombe-in-the-Moor, Dartmoor.

Corfe Castle in Dorset is dominated by its dramatic castle ruins.
Opposite: the sun rises over sandy Boscombe beach near Bournemouth.

Golden hamstone and thatched cottages are characteristic of Hinton St George, Somerset.

Rocky pinnacles face the Atlantic swell at Porth Moina, near Land's End, West Cornwall.

A Dorset thatcher at work. England has more thatched buildings than anywhere else in Europe.

Engine houses of the Crown Mines, Botallack, West Cornwall. The tin workings here extended for more than half a mile under the sea.

A statue of Richard Hooker, co-founder of the Anglican religious tradition, outside Exeter Cathedral.
Opposite: St Germans viaduct over the River Tiddy, southeast Cornwall.

An oat crop ready to harvest on Cranborne Chase, Dorset.

The Circus in Bath. The architect John Wood wanted to keep the link with the city's Roman past, so this parade of townhouses, completed in 1768, echoes the Colosseum in Rome.

Surfers enjoy a muted sunset at Watergate Bay, Newquay, north Cornwall.

Opposite: the beach huts at Hengistbury Head near Christchurch in Dorset are eagerly sought after.

A scarecrow guards a gate near Colliford Reservoir on Bodmin Moor.
Opposite: bluebells carpet woodland at Pendarves near Camborne, mid Cornwall.

Along the coast from Lynton to the Valley of Rocks, Exmoor, north Devon.

Inquisitive calves on the Lizard Peninsula, West Cornwall.

Smeaton's Tower on Plymouth Hoe, Devon.
The lighthouse was moved from Eddystone Rock in 1882.

Towards the distant tors of Dartmoor, from Mardon Down near Moretonhampstead.

English stonecrop thrives on an old stone wall at Porlock Weir, Exmoor.

Opposite: through an arch to the sea at Tintagel Castle, north Cornwall. The castle's Arthurian links are hotly debated.

High tide in the harbour at Lyme Regis, west Dorset. The port's heyday was in the 17th and 18th centuries.

In the footsteps of miners, excise men and prehistoric farmers on a footpath to Porth Moina, near Zennor, west Cornwall.

Charles' Church, Plymouth was destroyed by German bombing in 1941. It's now a memorial to the 1,172 civilians who died in the city's blitz.

Sand patterns at sunrise on the beach at Sandbanks, near Bournemouth.

Fields of yellow oilseed rape, south of Chard, Somerset.

Gateway to Bickleigh Castle, a 14th-century fortress by the River Exe, Devon.

An ancient gateway on Exeter's Cathedral Green.
Opposite: Brunel's Royal Albert Bridge and a modern road bridge span
the Tamar, linking Plymouth in Devon with Saltash in Cornwall.

Fruit flourishes in the Eden Project's Warm Temperate Biome.

Opposite: the Eden Project's biomes are vast unique greenhouses set in a disused Cornish quarry.

Rock climbers tackle the huge granite mass of Haytor, Dartmoor.

A pilot gig beached in St Ives, west Cornwall. Originally used for servicing ships at anchor, these fast, six-oared rowing boats are now raced by clubs all over western England.

A hawthorn tree on an ancient track near Dartmeet, Dartmoor.

Tintagel's massive cliffs add drama to a place of Arthurian legend.

Sea kayaks come ashore on the long sweep of sand at Woolacombe, north Devon.

Pulteney Bridge, Bath, northeast Somerset, one of only a handful of its kind in Europe to be lined with shops.

A quiet bench in the National Trust's Trelissick Garden, Feock, mid Cornwall.
Opposite: the Huers' Hut, Newquay, north Cornwall, once sheltered a lookout
for the pilchard shoals on which the local fishing fleet depended.

Mist hangs in the field on a chilly morning in east Dorset.

Exeter's Cathedral can trace its origins to Saxon times.

Low tide in St Ives' harbour. The town took off as a resort with the arrival of the railway in 1877.

Parson Hawker's Hut, Morwenstow, north Cornwall. The eccentric 19th-century clergyman would retire here to smoke opium and watch the sea.

Begun in 1880, Truro's Gothic Revival-style cathedral was the first 'new' cathedral in England since Salisbury, 800 years previously.

Colourful wellies for splashing in the sea at Fowey, southeast Cornwall.

St Ives Head, west Cornwall, shelters the bay from the open Atlantic beyond.
Opposite: Bodmin Moor in Cornwall is littered with ancient remains, but Showery Tor's
granite balancing act is a natural phenomenon.

Through the arch to Trim Street, Bath. Built in 1707 it was one of the first of Bath's 'new' streets, breaking out from the medieval city.

Yachts fill the River Dart between Kingswear and Dartmouth, south Devon.

A Dartmoor pony and its foal graze beneath Haytor, Dartmoor.
Opposite: Swanage's Victorian pier, a good place to start exploring the Jurassic Coast of east Dorset.

Waterfalls at Watersmeet, near Lynmouth, Exmoor, where the East Lyn river tumbles down a series of narrow gorges to the sea.

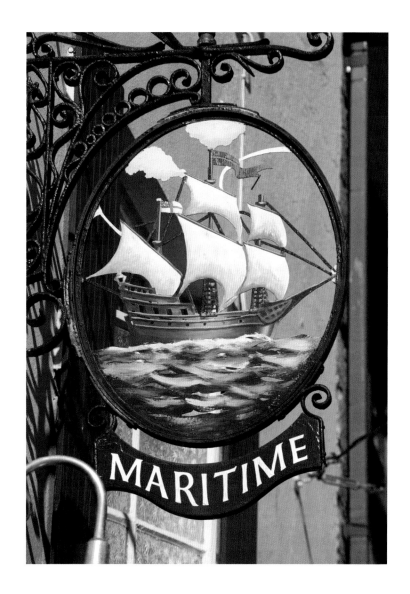

A pub sign in the heart of Plymouth's Barbican, the city's old harbour district.

The mouth of the River Exe in south Devon is popular with windsurfers.

Climbing on the dramatic sea cliffs above Porth Moina, west Cornwall.

Incoming tide races under the suspension bridge to Towan Island, Newquay, mid Cornwall.

The Roman Baths in the city of Bath. The city's original hot springs still attract thousands of visitors every year.

*Mên an tol, Morvah, west Cornwall, a curious granite
megalith which may once have been part of a stone circle.
Opposite: Torquay's new inner harbour bridge and tidal sill.*

The sun sets beyond Godrevy Island and its lighthouse, near Hayle, west Cornwall.

The Bristol Channel and the distant Welsh coast can be seen from heather-clad Dunkery Beacon, Exmoor's highest point.

Long horned highland cows graze the edge of Colliford Reservoir on Bodmin Moor, Cornwall.
Opposite: Plymouth's Tinside Lido, now restored to its Art Deco glory.

Highcliffe Castle, near Christchurch, east Dorset. The mansion dates from the 1830s and is a popular venue for weddings.

The huge pebble bank of Porlock beach, Exmoor.

71

A glimpse of Whipsiderry beach, near Newquay, mid Cornwall.

Zennor church, west Cornwall, where even the legend of a mermaid seems plausible.

Just walking the dog at Watergate beach, Newquay.
Opposite: a line of beach huts out of season at Boscombe, east Dorset.

Garden flowers poke through a fence at Studland, east Dorset.

Sidmouth, east Devon, John Betjeman's 'feast of visual delight'.

Learning to surf on Porthmeor Beach, St Ives, west Cornwall.

At Golitha Falls, near Liskeard, southeast Cornwall, the River Fowey cascades through ancient oak and ash woodland.

The Tate St Ives – a national gallery to recognise the importance of the 'St Ives School' of artists.

Cliffs and stacks of unusual serpentine rock make Kynance Cove, southwest Cornwall, fascinating and spectacular.

Cornflowers flourish in the Valley of Rocks, near Lynton, Exmoor.
Opposite: Lizard Point is England's most southerly point.

Porthcurno Beach in west Cornwall is a glorious stretch of golden sand close to Land's End.

Padstow, north Cornwall, is a welcome harbour for sailors on a notoriously rocky coast.

On the ramparts of Totnes Castle, south Devon, originally one of King Alfred's defences from the 10th century.

Roses cling to a cottage wall in Bossington, near Porlock, Exmoor.

Evening primroses flourish in the fragile dunes of Dawlish Warren, south Devon.

A large tortoiseshell butterfly lands on buddleia,
or butterfly bush, in Berwick St John, Wiltshire.

Berry Pomeroy Castle, south Devon. Deserted since the 17th century, it has retained many architectural styles.
Opposite: the rock arch of Durdle Door opens on to a pristine beach on Dorset's 'Pleistocene Coast'.

'Mirror' class dinghies racing at Fowey, southeast Cornwall.

Despite its ruinous state, Berry Pomeroy Castle in Devon is still an intriguing sight.

Collecting pebbles at Millook, near Crackington Haven, north Cornwall.
Opposite: early morning mist surrounds the broken teeth ruins of Corfe Castle.

INDEX